# Furnace Harbor

PHILIP D. CHURCH

# Furnace Harbor

*A Rhapsody of
the North Country*

\*

UNIVERSITY OF ILLINOIS PRESS

URBANA AND CHICAGO

Publication of this work was made possible in part by grants from the
National Endowment for the Arts and the Illinois Arts Council, a
state agency.

This book is printed on acid-free paper.

Library of Congress Cataloging-in-Publication Data

Church, Philip D., 1935–
    Furnace harbor: a rhapsody of the north country/
Philip D. Church.
        p.   cm.
    ISBN 0-252-06003-2 (alk. paper)
    I. Title.
PS3553.H83F8    1988
813'.54—dc19

                                    87-27229
                                         CIP

*Ann Arbor, Michigan*
*and Gambier, Ohio*

\*

*for Barbara, and Terry,*
*and for Radcliffe Squires*

# Headpieces

\*

From the shadow of the prehistoric world emerge dying religions that have not yet invented gods or goddesses, but live by the mystery of the elemental powers in the universe, the complex vitalities of what we feebly call Nature.

—D. H. Lawrence

The Word at rest rests in the mind in the restless continuation, the breaking down of all internal continual, the interruption of persistent locomotion, the persistent irruption of volcanic inconsequence. The landscape revised to portray a reality. . . .

Then all windings and peels, all rushings on, all streams out of springs we do not know where, all rush of senses and intellect thru time of being—lifts me up; as if out of the pulse of my bloody flesh, the gasp of breath upon breath (like a fish out of water) there were another continuum, an ever-purling stream, crystal and deep, down there, but a flow of water.

—Robert Duncan

Es hob sich eine Woge heran im Vergangenen . . .

(A wave from the things of the past rose toward you . . . )
—Rilke

And if I speak of principles, when there are none, I can't help it, there must be some, somewhere.
—*Malloy*

To live is a sacred manner.
—Algonquin

Yron passid thorgh his saule.
—Hampole *Psalter*

# Contents

*

# Foreword

*

"Furnace Harbor" is Fayette, Michigan, located on a peninsula that extends off the southern shore of the Upper Peninsula, three-quarters of the way across from Mackinaw to the Wisconsin border. Fayette opens on to Big Bay de Noc, in Lake Michigan and nearly at the head of Green Bay. It was a notable producer of pig iron from about 1875 to 1891, when the furnaces were shut down due to competition, shipping costs, and the shortage of hardwood used to kiln charcoal for the blast furnaces.

Development of Fayette began in 1864 when the Jackson Iron Company determined to expand on the profits and demand created by iron production during the Great Conflict. Later, Fayette flourished through the demand for iron and steel created by the western expansion. The deep harbor, the abundance of hardwood, the great limestone bluff, and, of course, the ready availability of iron ore made Fayette a likely site.

But, in fact, it was an ironworks in the wilderness and so foredoomed by increasing competition from the great iron and steel centers of the Midwest. When I visited Furnace Harbor in 1962, it was a ghost town in ruins, overgrown by trees and underbrush, a relic. The State of Michigan had just then begun the work of restoration, and Fayette is now a popular state park and historical site.

In its heyday, about five hundred people lived and worked there, in a company town. Many of the men were married, with families, a fact that the poem ignores, as it ignores the baseball team, the cornet band, and the "Opera House." But, married or single, their lives were hard. The "Hotel" and the "Boarding House" were for the single workers, and except for the ironworks themselves, were the largest structures. I remember reading about Mr. Sleet's brothel, but cannot at present locate the source.

The Laurentian Range, which exposed the iron and copper deposits along the northern shore of the Upper Peninsula, especially in the Keweenaw Peninsula and at Marquette and Ishpeming, is in fact the original land that rose from the waters to create the North American continent. The whole region is very sparsely populated, generally a relic of history, and retains its character as a wilderness. The strong impression it creates of timeless origins, and of history "past" yet "present," was the inception of the poem.

In the poem, Lake Superior is often referred to when, in geographic fact, Lake Michigan must be the referent. This particular poetic license is certified by the omnipresence in the North Country of its most truly fearsome sea—Superior. Cross Village was an Indian settlement in the Lower Peninsula, about twenty miles south of the Straits of Mackinac. The Indian painting was—and I trust still is—along the coast between Escanaba and Fayette.

The iron made at Furnace Harbor was charcoal-smelted pig. No conversions were milled there. The pigs were shipped south to Cleveland and other Great Lakes ports. Mr. Fayette Brown, who developed the works, was a Clevelander. The author grew up in a small steel town between Youngstown and Warren, Ohio.

# I

## THE BUOY

*Overture*

\*

*D*ong dong. Dong. In-
*tones the bell buoy*
*tongue-tied to the bottom*
*of the mouth of the bay;*
*measuring the interstices*
*eyeballed from headland*
*to headland, striations*
*of sandstone, limestone,*
*fir, pine, birch,*
*migrations of roots,*
*sea-currents, copper*
*veins, furs and pelts*
*of the herds, the pairs,*
*the loners, the keels*
*of grounded ships, or*
*sunk: your iron-*
*linked umbilical, buoy,*
*circles, twists, in*
*the rise and falls*
*of your navalgray*
*belly, red-striped;*
*tongue pitted, slung*
*upon an arc of pulse, sway,*
*slung to the sand bottom,*
*sandstone, limestone, granite*
*shelves all down the ledges*
*down the sides of the world.*

\*

I came here to witness
a restoration, and turn
arrested by you, your

Dong   Dongdong

Dong

that marks the channel.
Where, O mother, father,

where was your
beginning?

                *

You lift and fall, lift, ride
and slip in the pull, (down) the
crease, through corridors of gray
inland sea, harbor-headed, stone-
swung, bound home to home
as the oil-slicked, borne sailor
at watch aboard his lake's ship
went down with the lights
of Chicago, Petoskey, Menomenee
sunk in the hull-down steerages
of his eyes.
                Rolling over, her
undersea belly, ship adrift
in the heaviest of coldest seas,
sinking within lantern sight,
cannon-shot, or lost hands of land,
her bell still ringing down there,
her brave, brass ship's bell
chiming lanyard-strung the
dong-dong-dong-dong . . . dong
of the going down, rolling,
in her slow vaginal twistings,
the spiraling down into her one
seascaped burial, the sea-groined,
caverned hull. The bobbing channel
buoy mocks or mimics, marks
and sounds her breaking.
Glacier-bedded, brass-bound
granite-faced beloved of the
lost sister, whose hands
flow untouchable as fawn's fur,
silent, soft as incest.

                They tell that
the bells of lost ships chime

the northern hours like snow,
and if you listen you can hear
all a winter's night their bells
ringing in the blindy waters
off Ludington and Manistique.

Buoy, you ripple home this
sun-shot, serene, fall afternoon
over Furnace Harbor all the lost
ships swaying home-dreaded
beneath you, cargoed as mothers,
benign and rust-seamed
as an old father's fallen,
birth-lined buttocks.
In the sun's flash, turning,
your ruststains shine
into blood . . . like mine.
Mine? Blood, or rust,
it isn't yours, or mine.
No blood belongs to us.

⁂

*Coiling links of rusted chain;*
*greased, steel-wire hawsers;*
*lines cast splashing vortices off sterns,*
*where (glass, limestone, sand striations)*
*twin screws boil and foam, make*
*way as the water ripples, sucked*
*in and under, yields, gathers*
*against its own yielding pressure,*
*like flesh, like flame in the air,*
*like needles of fir, like a finger*
*worked into loam, like waxen*
*flame, the cold, sharp burn*
*in the eye, seen in the eye*
*when your eye bends close*
*to a heat, a source,*
*too close for comfort.*

*

I construct a compass of driftwood,
a compass rose, fire it, and noon
rises white light in my eyes, circling,
swirling up and away,
as the buoy darkens across the bay,
corkscrews, topples off sun-shot crest
to crest. I near-rhyme that image with my
sex. Though here is an image of all
fathering, all mothering, in all lips
of tongued speech, or wombed, or naveled—
umbilicaled unravelings of the twisted lines
out the ribbed and boned chambers of mouths;
porpoise, whale, seal articulations, liquid lipped.

So, the rotting iron chains, anchored
or buried in bottom sand, or caught,
secured to cleat, chock, or windlass,
belly and coil, drive down; then drift,
lapse—then drawn down a tidal
shift, a sudden current, they lift,
haul, tighten, explode like the crack
of a whip (all down there, in dark
water, hear!) like a rifle's percussion,
recoil, shock, like a snake strikes,
that cold, fanged flame that numbs,
and the snake, the great chain, draws
back, stunned by its own blind hit,
wavers there in its lapsing—sexual—
as smoke caught curls back down
the grooved channels of its own barrel,
or the supper's smoke, wind swung,
coils back down its chimney, pitiless:
where the huddled family bends in its
comfort of hearth, while the numbed
bullet strikes the cold flesh of . . .

my fire darkens with the afternoon.

What do I see in there, remembering,
that it all passes away so vividly?
What do we see, in this solitary
combustion? This harbor of furnaces.
Offshore, the sun-shot buoy, riding its shadows
in a lengthening swell, tolls and tolls
brightly, darkly, some glottal story,
as if sounds alone might make a plot.
Here, I am all at once lost entirely.
The fire, the stones, the bay, the buoy.
In an instant, all memories form, disappear.
They rise and flow and sink. Fire to water.
The last sense is heard: silence,
with that weight and pressure.

A child over again, I sound myself.
Something invisible that hits. Fallen
I see you, old father, spiral, fall.
Going down, I bear all your dead weight.
Keeled and cargoed, sealed-hatched and
laddered down the lanterns of your hold.
And I haul you up, daddy, and shove
you overboard, into the black harbor
of your dreams. I hear the splash.

I watch your ghost or strange form
come back up again, in and out that
yellow winter window in Youngstown, Ohio,
drowning through steel mills of nitrogens,
sulfur, all hell's slag dumps
and the neon heart of the Victory Grill.
I bear you so much more love than ill-will,
all I can remember are images: waiting
for you off some broken sidestreet
I can't even remember—Prospect Avenue,
was it? Briar Hill? The red rain.

Dark father, I think on you, now,
and honor the unregistered cargoes of your

regret, neglect, and servitudes, that weighed
you to your sinking, stately love of women.
I recover you, the gentleman in the wrong bar,
so originally American you never understood
what in hell the rest of us were thinking.
Though to this moment, I cannot answer the questions
in your eyes, that were so deeply brown I
see them now as obsidian, still fired.
I let you go now, in all love's farewell.
I am a father now, too, daddy. I yield
for the both of us, fear. Let us be.

   *

All that afternoon, caught
in the rise and fall, dull
ringing or donging, the *dong*
of the bell buoy hooked and
tongued drifting in circles
down the channel of Furnace Harbor,
I saw them all, all breaths
wide, furred, eyes staring,
drowned, round whites like
fishbellies of chalk penis-flesh
swaying, circling round and round
the stone, boned hip's groin or grin,
the hair slicked seal-smooth
across the high forehead, liftings
of bone, hair over bone . . .
lost fathers, lost sons, lost
ships, and the palms of women.

Then, the rising of fathers, flesh-furled.
The mother, stone-downed, rising.
In the winter night, the belly rising
with you, father-son, like dough.
Yet here, the fire, the noon, barren.
The light holds, will not fall.

*

And these cliffs of limestone,
their darkened trees rooted in stone,
call them out. I am not remembering,
I see. In the silences between
dong       dong       dong
see your eyes lifting into mine.
Cold, your fingers brush me,
and pull me down. I kneel
on the stones that slip and
topple me home, that chalk me
with the lime of your tonguing.
I shall bear down, shall bear
round stone after stone from
this fire to the harbor's ebb,
and let them go, each one,
down, down, to strike the bottom,
to roll and strike again, sounding,
until, sunken, sunken, I
sound.

         Until, beached at last
in my own childish hefting and
carting, and stripped like a limb
white and wet, stupid with
this trundling and rolling of stones,
spent, I kneel where the
surface catches, slides, lets go.
At the water's surface I hear,
Indian as my father, bone-faced,
I feel tomorrow's snow coming
across Canada, from the poles,
five, six, seven hundred miles off,
coming in over this land-sea,
across this water. I catch
the white combers coming in.
I smell the land rise beneath
this inland, island sea,
the ghostly bows of a great

ship all whirled and whorled
in snow, in white rain, like
the blind prow of blind fatherings
come to grind and batter its keel
into the granite shelves of your ice.
Chains rattling bottomless
through the deadheads of her eyes.

So, the drowned sailors twist and turn,
lift and let fall the red-flaked
bell buoy of all sailing channels,
as my eyes clear, and I watch
the buoy in its forlorn forewarnings,
and open my nostrils to vegetation
that, unleaved and made bone, breathes
for me. I open my mouth to
sea-wind, sand, lime, drift-pine,
and handy among the sea-wrack,
reconstruct my stone-scattered fire,
replace the rocks and limbs
and light a fire.

Though I will wait
long for that fire
to burrow home
as veins spiraling
heat into heart's heat,
as stone into stone,
into bone, loam.
Murmured by the cold
chain-links of the
bell buoy, that
lifts and falls,

            Dong-dong
                to mark the channel.

*

The fire lit, all but invisible
but lit, built, wavering,
banked, and mine, me.
I slide my fingers round
rocks sea-borne and steaming;
they roll and burn and cut,
channeling. Rock and log
and sawed ice like teeth
and vegetable flesh and bone.

So here's my fire, cold-cocked,
smoldering, sinking, tongue-
turned, stone-breaking, for
an Indian breaking granite to
hammer, hammer, pure copper into
sunbursts
              and bowls.

So, sea-headed, here's my spear,
milky in the fire-lit sand,
like bone chips for the kindling.

Look, here I am, blood
and bone, both, a belly's brain
with a memory for salting.
Salt water and the fishskin
eyeballs where the world
curves into darkness and waves,
90° east, spinning,
downwind the Lincoln Sea;
46° north, American
this instant, until spun
I am whirled away.

          *

I watch the waves come right on in.
Downwind, here, tidal, where the

compass spins. They come all the way in,
underground, as once seas of ice
traversed the ground, as far inland as
Tennessee, I imagine: moraines, Indian
mounds, bone-burials, earth-
sculpted seascapes of the solstices
shaped like falcons and the wavering rings
of trees, like the whorls or figurings
of wounds washed in rivers, earth-
blood, ore, copper—it was copper,
not bronze, they beat into sunbursts,
for the explosions of the sun were
already in the copper, granite-groined.
Earth-water, rust, flint, and iron.
Furnace Harbor: the fleshheat of earthmounds,
as corn underground, fired,
and the Indian bones
that yellow, encircled,
turn ivory.

Wading out, now, the inland tide
sways me, out and back, up
and down. My feet drift seaward
ripple to ripple, nudged, urged
by lake pressure, a kernel, a
drift, loins and belly, and no
matter how solidly I plant my feet
sea-currents lean through the ground,
sway and urge, forward and back.
But always by the buoy fastened
I dance to the sand stone-bottomed.

                *

In pitch darkness,
water warm as lymph,
at my nose, into it,
in my mouth, in my ears,
a washing, draining
lubrication, rhythmic

blind baptisms of lift
and fall, the bell buoy
ringing in the blackness
just ahead, weird brother
skinned or drowned yet
circling, swaying, sounding
for me my immaculate
conceptions—

                The milky flow
at night, in certain algae
in the Gulf of Mexico like
porpoise milk, the foam
which was my genital-forming.
But now, here at Michigan,
it is my nostrils, my mouth,
my ears that twist and form
to an older pitch and swell
than Mexico or salt water.
The great northern breast
of the Earth, blue-veined,
and the madonna meat
of the limestone shadows. Here
I am witness to my
own conception, and of my
birthing, with all the times
of my bodies drawn to a poise,
a shift, and swaddling night.
A foam of limestone, shadow
of fir and furs, a rock of
seagirthed ponderous
suck beyond any gulf
or harbor or island shelf.
"Superior never gives up
her dead" because,
continent, ice
ocean, sea of ice,
sexless as a sword of ice,
blue in a green vault of ice,

glacial, moon-bellied,
Superior holds all births
in its thunderous chastity,
and sculpts its outer lips
into the pure relics of things
petrified into their acts of dying.
The tides pull so deep,
twist so tight, only your
bones hear, remember.

   *

Tides
swell and sink
where no tides are, draw.
Inland, this sea sucks a
continent four cold lakes away,
suspending it, like plasma.
There is the one pressure, here,
draws down all rivers rising.
its buoy lifts and forever falls,
down and down, down, down,
spiraling the globe,

      etching the channel.
      Grooves it home.

   *

So roll, buoy, your

      red-rust-stained-gray belly, your
chaste articulations of lift and fall,
old dong, and
     dong  dong
        ringing
    home your neat notations,
    measured in stately equations,
    insinuating something whole—
ride, sideslipping, revolving

like a slick fin, vestigial tongue, into
one terrible black hole

O

from mine-darkness to cliff cavern,
to my Indian burial.

# II

## THE RESTORATION

*First Movement*

\*

Young men, half-naked, bronzed,
move here about the ironwork's
restoration.
                    Big-muscled kid,
there's nothing to restore here, the
restoration is complete in ribbed
bottom-sand, pine vaults, sun-shot
limestone cliffs,
                    in equations
                              of fire and shadow,
                              water and blood.


Restoration is a flat stone skipped
across bay water, ripple to ripple. Once,
twice, three times and then it cants, diving,
curving into water, sideslips round,
and round, down, like a leaf
drifting down, sinking
seeded deep into loam,
etched into seed, shell.
Quartz vein through granite,
copper or burnished bronze,
pure vein in shattered stone
the old Indians exploded
in the caves of cliffs, firing
the chunks of pried granite,
dashing them with cold water,
cracking them open, and then
prying out pure copper, hammering it
into sunbursts, bowls, eagles
serpent-tongued, hearts'
knives breastblooded
in Mexico.


                    Dark-breasted, a boy bows his back,
his flesh swells in halves, his spine
knobbed and naked, his eyes caught
in a flash of women. You, young worker,
straighten mid-hammer-swing to stare at

me and two women as we trail past you,
carting to the far point our stuff of a picnic.
Boy, you stand up and stare, caught, frozen there,
in a longer procession of the newly dead and laid
than your burnt flesh has yet confessed to you.

        I see about us, about the walls of
        shattered buildings, cliffs and forest,
        in the thin light of this northern sun
        what this restoration
        comes down to:

Burial-mounds (Aztec-altars, black-blood)
the clear whites of a boy's eyes, the flash of
white flesh the girls' skirts let fly, the shadowings of
all-watching Eye, peel of whiteflesh behind the kiln where
quickly (whispering "hurry, hurry") one twists loins free,
sun bursts off two quick bellies, knived. . . .

We're past, and he turns away, humming his hammer.
And I could tell him to plant his feet parallel, swing
that twelve- or sixteen-pounder in one continuous circle,
not to bend and lift, bend and lift, straighten and plunge.
But it doesn't matter how he hits the stone, or
        hammers home against home,
there is no restoration he can hammer alone
at Furnace Harbor:
        The buoy rings out a clear
                Dong.    Dong.
                        You untwine your legs, your eyes
             all gone, swelling,
                    circling round
        the buoy's rusty belly,
        the turn and toss of
        ships and flashing lights
        off the headland.
        The flash of deer

across the headlights—
rock, trees, fur,
fire, flesh,
limestone.

# III

## THE CLIFFS

*

On the limestone cliffs
down the seaward wall
at the windward escarpment
above a shale beach slick and
no more than one-half stride from the seawall
to the surf which pounds here always at high tide,
in faded pigments—orange, blue, off-red—
is drawn a child's picture or symbol of the sun
beside a stick figure of a man
simplified as archeological Indian
with a truly remarkably long dong
pissing long and strong
straight into the sun.

*

Two drunken Indians
drew and colored them here—
stick-donged man and Aztec sun—
on the limestone cliff,
prehistorically, by hand,
just after the ice waves grooved the rock
with monotonous stoned fingers into
the Straits of Mackinac, where later,
*voyageurs* for the greater glory of god
canoed theology and empire and courage
across the inland sea toward India.
*Old fathers, fare ye well: voyaging—*
*O you who crossed the seas*

and hit Green Bay, where the Stinkers roasted you
pigs and ignored your kimonos, Father Nicolet,
and the farts of your two French pistols. Some
months later, all the little Stinkers
sang: "Father, Father Nicolet,
Sailed for Indi, hit Green Bay.
In his gorgeous robes of clay,
Our pale Father could not stay."

\*

Two drunken Indians, I was
saying, sailed headlong
into that cliff, hit it and yawed,
eyes still set, staring far ahead,
paddles digging, deep-thrusting: hit
again, the prow rising, ship-shuddering—
on their way home from St. Ignace via
Cross Village on the lower peninsula
where the cousin and girlfriend of the one
lived with the sister and ex-wife of the other,
manufacturing, distributing, and merchandising
from Dearborn and Ann Arbor to Duluth
birchbark teepees and canoes, chicken-feather war bonnets,
deerskin loinclouts of rabbit hide, bagged balsam
(aphrodisiac), pine-needle pincushions with the
Real Smell of the Original Old North Country,
sandstone arrowheads, rubber-tipped True Blue arrows,
Chippewa Chief Hair and Body Lubricating Solvent
and Aromatic Lotion, plastic love-beads, wampum,
Confederate two-dollar bills, Asiatic Totem Poles,
Alaskan agates eight thousand years old,
bear claws salvaged from runaway coonhounds,
a half-eaten pasty one century old—
half eaten by the first Black miner
in Hancock, Michigan, Big Willie,
seven-feet-six-inches tall who
lost two hundred pounds in one week
and died drunk and murderous of swamp fever
at the age of thirty-two—

one lacrosse stick
stained with real blood from the Massacre at
Michilimackinac, 1763, and other things:
a photo of the ironmen,
gallused and bum-booted,
standing ranked like conscripts
at their company fish fry, stare

of black-holed eyes like whipped sons,
forked men split between boyhood
and derelict age, mother-haunted,
father-lost. The abandoned battalion,
the sagged, stink-panted infantry
of the North Woods, the Company:
"Line up, fall in, you goofers!"
Their stringy necks, these photographs, these
hammers, belt buckles, leathers
green as their flesh, survive.
*God keep them.*

       *

So they set forth, these Indians,
canoeing home to Escanaba, their twin
blades rising, falling, trailing moon-
and star-bright droppings, the sea
a silver shimmer in widening wake, their
earthenware jug secured abaft the leeward gunwale,
merchandise and contraband lashed fore and aft.
Their shoulders hump—rising, falling—
heads lifted and slightly canted, yet
steady into the wind, their beady eyes jet
black, gleaming like half-cooked liver.
They course, tack and beat, through the
starlit, moon-tracked, fragrant, and
starkissed main, lost in the rhythms
of paddle, ocean, swell, and surf drumming,
rhythm of bowed backs rising, falling, their
paddles thrust deep into darkness, the long,
slow, steady pull, then quickly lifted,
the droplets like mercury across velvet,
their necks stretched out like thoroughbreds,
their nostrils flared like Whirlaway,
their assholes sprouting bristles. . . .

                             They hit,

they hit that rockwall cliff

like stepping stark-staring blind into a midnight tree.
Their eyes wide, still staring upwind, still
hot in rhythm, paddles still going strong,
sucking air, they hit that cliff head on
like an arrow from out of the night
whocks into the headboard of your bedstead,
like a daddy running-up a kite hits
his own car, parked in an open field. . . .
hits so hard it's two minutes spinning
before his nose starts to bleed. And you,
O proud-crested bow, you rose bravely
as the chests of chargers at Cemetery Ridge rose
and took the shock, like a rake handle in the balls
long after midnight. They hit, slewed, took water,
hit again and the current, that tricky subterrestrial current
caught their stern and swung her wide, the slim ship,
the well-wrought craft: and stunned,
the longship swings athwart, rocks side to side
like a gut-shot moose, and hits again,
this time splintering the lee rail,
and all her hatches springing . . . O.

Through their red haze the Indians behold
sea serpents writhe, flash like trout,
blossom as sea anemones are said to blossom
adrift coral in Mexican seas. "Mother of pearl!"
one cries, dazzled adrift, starry-eyed,
dawning to dazzle the crystal vortices of eyes,
their richnesses of long, intricate spiralings
of blood, coagulating tendrils of roots,
spiraling like sperm through cold water,
his teeth mashed, his nostrils snorting gouts of blood
redder than desert prophet's red rock.
And the ship subsides, water-wallowing now,
drifting sinkage along the cliffside,
rocking gently in the eddying tide,
like a stoved schooner in a drainage ditch.

The first Indian holds fast,

nose flowing rock-communion
with those drowned, not past.

His friend, second-in-command, budding
artist, though of the same earnest age,
lifts toward his painting, rapt with symbol.
He chooses off-red, burnt orange, aquamarine.

His captain, ballast of the poop deck, holds
steady their craft, exquisite though badly bunged,
rides her steady in the inland tide,
and braces himself, hands to limestone, feet-splayed.
Up the artist reaches, measures, slowly as a genius,
traces and paints first that remarkably long dong,
then sketches in one reverse-jointed leg,
and then, in whirling pigments, the sun!
But his captain, it must have been about then,
goes aft to piss off the taffrail downwind

and God! and Lo!

paint, painter, pots, and piss fly!
The cunning-crafted, slim-ribbed canoe
squishes away, rolls drunken, like two
carp fornicating in a finger-bowl.
The painting Indian, nearly through the sun
and with one leg and the dong on his stick man,
grabs hold, strung out there upon the face of stone
like Jesus Christ, and hangs on
with that last, desperate, horned and yellowed toe
to the sweetly curved, steam-curled, gently,
lovingly planed and fashioned hardwood gunwale.
He's strung out there like crowbait to windward,
twanging between rock and water
against the limestone cliff face,
like a weathering goat hide
or rigid, plastered saint,
still daubing aquamarine, off-red, burnt orange,
working each pigment into the pores of stone.

Now the head is done, and now the first arm.
Then the Captain-pisser circles back toward the poop deck,
and the goddamned craft, the ship, that unkeeled,
snakebellied thing
        tilts again, heels right over,

*and* the snap, the tear of the painter's crotch
echoes off rock and water as a rifle shot
ricochets, sharp as the zilch of Fate, blunt as
truth, ragged yet sustained as Confederate musket fire,
till that pisser gets back to his post, leaving a
neat, cadenced figure eight of piss,
point by point, in military array,
clean across the decks.
"Will you for pleased Christ's sake stand still?"
Asked quietly, quietly, no
exclamation point, no, but
with just that slight rising
inflection on the final three
syllables that suggest, but barely, barely
hysteria, the rise and fall of Caesars. . . .
But, sloshed, the ship's adrift, the damage done,
and lunging, the Captain-pisser grabs for leg, dong,
thigh, navel, anything on the quivering guy wire
of his painting friend, to grab, hold, to save
any part or port of him, glottis, lip, nostril,
nipple, navel, knee, before his fork splits.

Captain misses with an arm,
misses again with a last-ditch, hooking leg,
and Lord! the damned ship tips again in the backwash,
and legs, arms, breechclouts, wampum,
wine bottles, paddles, prophylactics,
teepee samples, ragdolls, pucks, and paint,
three gross of rubber-tipped arrows,
two Old Milwaukees and one catfish on rye
drift away, sink, sideslipping down
like homesick stone, or
the knotted, full condom,

ribbed, transcendent, that
bottom bumps and drifts submarine
back and forth the floors of the Great Lakes
forever, like some paleolithic lure,
cunning decoy of those translucent worms,
lunarshining, one-eyed, that loom
and disappear again down the deepest
valleys of the Indian Ocean,
or the bottomless Blue Hole
in Castalia, near Fostoria, Ohio,
of which the advertised one—
they claim it actually *is* bottomless—
at Indian Lake, near Manistique,
Michigan, twenty-three miles from
Furnace Harbor—is, like the condom,
a fabrication of man's duplicity, his
wishful thinking.

      *

Nonetheless,
two heads of hair (black)
streaming like Aphrodites, rise again.
One Indian gets an arm
clamped round a wet head,
locked under a nose.

Two or three fingers in an open mouth,
and hangs on (teeth, palate, sinus). . . .
The other gets both arms
round a loin, works a leg up a spine,
around a neck, into hair, ear,
and one, big, yellow toe hooked
like a cock back to rock.
He hooks that baby in
like a claw.

They snatch the sandwich and the bait can
from out the fast-flowing moon-spangled tide. . . .
All the other stuff

sinks on down, except
a cask of lumberman's wine.

    *

Now hang on, man! We're sailing into the wind, here,
    homeward bound! Singing: Earth Angel,
Rock of Ages, O Wheel of Fortune, Marching through Georgia,
    Stars Fell on Alabama, Danny Boy,
On the Road to Mandalay, Tennessee Stud,
all the way in to Escanaba where

the wives wait, not without hope . . .
swigging coffee laced with Stinker home brew,
downing fried crab, whitefish curry, pasties.
"Hey, man, did you paint us?"
"Shee-it, we painted you."
Hands streaked with paint, salt, blood,
toenails stoved, coagulating,
proud to be sailors catapulting ripples,
cornering round rocks, living off urchin, lichen,
sea anemone, weeds, bass, pike, perch,
tilefish, pompano, orange roughy, Madagascar smelt
smelted in brine; home the long way
to the harbor where the wrinkled, flannel-bundled
wives wait, shading their eyes,
scanning horizons.

They came, by God, up through
Big Bay du Noc, back to Furnace Harbor.
Gay and grim, cold Indian
proud to be red, gone so long,
thought dead, or drowned surely,
now home again, a little stiff
with pride, distant-eyed, a
tad formal; half-frozen:

"Where you been?" "Market-
research and stone-painting, woman."
And it survives: of a man

with a monkey-tailed dong, pissing
long and strong, straight
into the sun.

# IV

## THE BAY

*First Strophe*

\*

I'm thinking, momentarily, of another place,
ambiguously sworded as home:
I think, *don't let that sullen*
*place bleed and weary away*
*the rest of your life. Let*
*the drowned cavort their*
*sutured grimaces. Let*
*them reinvent themselves*
*day by day, as they can.*

*

So, I look out, again,
over this unrestored bay,
all awry in memory,
over . . . what? . . . the oils,
the translucences, the . . .
*how bays embody us,*
*as though we arose*
*in their eddies, back*
*waters, hipped and shouldered*
*to their uncertain curvatures,*
*found fingers come in, ashore:*

Look what sprouted. And toes!
And the long, long tissue
shrinks into the hole, a tongue!
And it dances on the ribs
of the cavern! Probes.
But the forehead swells, too.
And for all it understands,
it forgets more. Something
gray as worms in there tolls
the tongue and shrouds the eye.
A strange, unbodied sound,
strange as dawn in a tomb,
shapes itself in the cavern
of the mind. *Time,* it mutters.
The one word most pitiless, pure.
The word that means nothing.

Except sometimes, secret
in the liquid night,
when we remember
the bays of our birthing,
where our lost sisters,
brothers, glow fish-eyed.
Then, *Time* means
everything: wait, come,
stay. Pulse and breath.

And each nerve ending remembers
what spirals from cell to cell, coils
through blood, tissue into tissue,
migrates teeth from stone, flows like
water to fern to reeds to finger.
And has trailed us all our ways
from slime mangrove swamp
to Eden and out, to here.

This evening, off Furnace Harbor,
freshwater seas wrung
glacier pure, polar spun,
the original cove deepens
clear as the eyes of children,
and yet is amniotic, electrical, signaling.

The funky buoy rounds like
mother, our best idea of her,
and rings steady as breath:
a woman's one response.
I believe that all women
remember what came before
even they were little girls.
Some man invented time.

⁎

The bay invents nothing, even
as sand-water sinks into limestone,
seed seeps through black hair,

filters into root, trunk to tree,
leaves, hands, nails, mind—ikons,
whatever words our mouths form,
shaping air down veined channels
are tongues, gilled: water-sucked,
eyes popping like grapes, membranes
of words mouthed, breast-
sucked, are bay-contained.
Seed-sown, all our words
flow into this water, this loam.
Fluting, channeling, they spiral:
hair or fur: male, female.
Moss-rooted, pelvic stoned,
tide-drawn, calm, clear,
volcanic-mouthed, we flow
back into this bay.

Old chaste womb, rocking
buoy, a tongue's empty belly,
a bay full of stones,
your cheekbones, brothers, sisters,
slick hair, scales, fur,
your eyeballs, pigments, hips
like limestone wings cast out
and flung spinning, to skip and
sideslip down, plane upon
plane, into Furnace Harbor.

\*

Listen to the sounds your
tongue forms; hear the muted cry?
I taste blood, well-ironed
salt and salt water, fresh-bayed.
Looking up through the eyeball
of this bay, through currents,
through flowing veins of sand, reeds, lily pads,
through the green-moss bottom curves
of buoy and the bay's curvature,
up to our water-headed, our sky-orbed,

cockeyed, pin-pricked hemisphere,
globed, moonswollen, thin-skinned
flash or flow of sky, exploding sun:
you say, "I never saw *this* before."
Open your eyes; water flows in.
Drowned, your eyes grow gills.
Like a drifting, shucked pearl, your
eyeball twists at the bitter end
of the bell buoy's anchored umbilical.
The colors in your eyes wash out,
your eyes drift and take root,
open wide, and dive,
sink, root, and lift again,
wavering in water,
every tendril many-eyed
like the spots along a trout's
side, or wings of butterfly.

Coral, moss, lichen,
pine needle, birch leaf,
fire. Ash. Sand. Ore.
Sandstone, drowned, iron-
downed, landlocked sea echoing
in the stone caverns of the skull;
ice-foam sinks into pine-gum,
words muffled in a bedroom,
glistening sweat, hair, bark;

and in a cold Carolina morning
the bell rings clear again,
upwards through pine catacombs,
shadows shot with frost on fields,
cabined or kitchened, the bell,
ringing, empties white water
like silt down the fall-line,
the delta-templed, muck-grottoed,
housed and streaming sockets
of old springs; rivers

drifting, sinking, silt-flow
of porous petrified log
grown filthy with bottomland,
rich in straw. Thaw.
Dunged crystal, melting
spring-smell, raking
thawed dung, earth-sponge:
shoveling what I shit
back to dry-dust, crop-ground.
(Coming back up north now)
Rusted, rich bell buoy,
stone-headed old vessel,
O lost ship, I hear
the wind ringing your
blind, brass bell—

        Dong-Dong-Dong

              Dong    Dong

                  to mark the channel.

Soundings. Calculations. A rhythm.
Wash of bays in the silences like rivers
after the engines stall upstream.
In Superior the drowned sailors
never surface, never rot, they
roll with the glacial currents
from ribbed sand to buried tree,
from iced, molten, sprung glacial
rock to buried mine-bays—
they roll down there
forever frozen, fiery.
And the bay, placid,
grows white as the albumen
of a shelled egg,
or the white of breast, the
white flash of the drowned girl's eye:

pearls of fishes' eggs,
laid cairns of stonefall—
long Lady of the Lake.

Now I can see clear
to the bottom, foetus-eyed,
wide-eyed, wild-eyed Indian, eyeballing,
the sun spiraling down through bays of
lake, yolk-embryo, wound, black ice,
chalk-semen tonguetailed
crystals, headland fires
firred, the shadows of the women's breasts
that crouch and rise and bend
against the sky, in the firelight
shadowings of pelvis, pitch-pine,
of sandstone that melts in fire,
of gum seeping, human hand
all ice, stone, fire.

Bay veined as limestone,
old ice, grown green and dim.
What is our flesh, then?
Milk—breast? soft ribs
folded, rib-bedded?
We're brown-tongued,
like this bay's sandspit,
shadowy, erect, and the
rib-cage swells of
tipped flesh.

O Mother of bay-waters,
slick, sucking belle! The
buoy rings your chaste begetting—
and placid, placid, you weave
this impervious, transparent shell,
this place, this
staying . . .

rooted and drifting,

watered and rung,
paradise of eye,
of clear, deep, round
water, stone sprung,
empty as sky
still upon snow,
silent as snow,
the ice beneath
the snow upon
the bay, the
dark waters
beneath ice and snow,
the night sky
bright about us
ghosts our
forms in
snow.

# V

## THE INHABITANTS

*Second Movement*

\*

Detroit sharpers hauled women in here
from Milwaukee—German and Polish
girls, blonde-haired, like the losers
in war, stripped. And Finnish girls,
and Swedish ones; Beautiful Blonde
Virgin Captives of the North Woods,
their sign read, Wild Rhine Maidens
Subdued For You. And a few
gypsies from Romania, and half-breed
Cherokee Chief's Daughters From
Memphis, the man said. Get Yours,
Cheap. Clean. New. Anne
of Escanaba, who brought us here,
told us this, and of her father
who escaped from prison three
miles from Furnace Harbor, 1943,
fled up the dunes and disappeared
forever into the second growth,
the husks of old logging camps,
the abandoned frame houses, fallen
chimney grottoes, root cellars,
sawdust bins and the shattered
hulks of ships, out there still
for all Anne knew.

                    *

Daughter, for all your Indian eyes,
you sink like a white stone
into Furnace Harbor.

Here, in the crystal bay,
I watch you sink and sway,
your dark hair goes pale

as your slender limbs waver
beneath me, your eyes turn free,
larger as you sink, green to amber,
opening, enlarging me

as you spiral down, away from me,
magnified in Furnace Harbor.

                    *


*Skip a flat rock*
*across the tide, watch*
*your child play at its side,*
*that she not fall headlong into*
*Furnace Harbor. A father crying out:*
*"No, she shall not fall headlong here!"*

Gray-white gull
sweeps by, gray-black
shadow, pine-ringed,
bright-morning-skied, over
water, over sand, into
a birch-stand, as an
escaped convict plunges
up the dunes into timber,
circling, circling.

As a circling cat in heat,
or wolf or coyote or worse,
a wolverine without a mate,
yellow-black-eyed, staring,
backtracking round the fire
I built again years later,
on the run, on the sand —
keeping just outside the dark
perimeter, swinging into it,
circling out in parabola, and
moving off to catch the wind again,
making sure, and then coming on in again,
but backing off from the smell, my
white-flesh stink, who watches your
blank, bright stare like snow
coming in the night through pine

into fire, silent as beasts
that bed restless as you
in the lonely weather,
bound to the center of
deer-nestings, rabbit-warmed,
where leaved and needled the
man masturbates his seed like
pulp into the bays of trees:

the night sky with eyes
like lynx, beyond the
circle of my fire, the
node of sex, yellow-eyed.
They watch you, like a hound.

Ghosts, too, from the pine and
birch, the shattered, fallen
masonry, mark you. They bob
and weave, steady as cat-eyes.
The girl beneath you, in sand,
closes her eyes, weaves, shifts,
and is gone. I, too, sinking,
feel I am sinking, into Furnace
Harbor, my breath and my wife's—
and all goes gull-winged, diving:
as an animal stalks us, circling.

*Furnace Harbor beds, rests*
*and rounds us like ghost limbs—*
*tide-limbs, time-roots, sand*
*that twines and takes and spirals*
*back into the mind of where we came from,*
*wide-eyed where we find us,*
*like ships, and words, this sex.*
*Everything that was, is*
*here, in this gathering*
*without solace, a kind of*
*peace.*

\*

In a cornfield in southern Ohio
two of us lay caked and spent,
watched frond upon frond of
the corn leaves go back
and forth, rasping like claws
sheathed, teethed, veed. . . .

Our breath like hot breeze,
fitful, the river between your
breasts, down my belly . . .
eyes pooled, emptied. . . .

We burrow or groove sand
as though the earth were
rising here beneath our
blanket and limbs, hips,
those peculiar jointures,
and how the earth curves
beneath us, I feel it arch
its back right through you.

\*

No rock, silt, or shale,
no sand, loam, or red lime-
stone, or bark-droppings,
pine needles or granite or
agate-stones, or copper:
no earth older than this
earth right here, nor nakeder
than this, our bedding and
bay-love, Barbara, pitched
like an intricate tent—
our angles flesh out
sky and its drumming, as
the gull-shadow crosses
the water again.

Surface tension sucks
fingers to the bone,
probes ears like a tongue,
wears away my gristle.
Bones grind bone to bone, to
rock, lime, limestone. I
am barely here, now, and hear
us coming back into ourselves.

There are no myths here.
We are among the inhabitants,
and that is all.
"Come and get it while it's
still hot and stinks good,
you homeless bare-assed
bastards," is the straw boss's
Furnace Harbor morningsong.

   *

Lake grouper, with a fat lip,
jellied down there, moves.
You move, in shadows within
shadows, frozen alive, still
you swell under water like
whaleflesh, your flagy fins
timed to the surface ripples,
eyes wide as an axed thigh,
pink as rain-washed wound,
gills bright as vagina:
opening, closing,
tolling, as the bell
tolls

  DONG DONG

      to mark the channel.

Swallowing, your great-
gummed mouth green-bubbled

with children, your scales
heavy with sons, biblical;
suspended, drifting, aye,
very like a fossil, eyes
wide and staring as a walleyed
pike's, deep-greened as muskie,
holding on down there,
breathing water, a poem
under verbal pressure,
weeded and whorled.

*In multiple, metric*
*spurts, multicolored,*
*resilient, brook trout shadowflash*
*rock to rock.*

\*

The creek runs
down to the bay.
The water is clear,
yet flows burnt orange
with iron, like rust.
All eyes are upon me
as I slip my hand
beneath a limestone,
for suddenly I love
the trout, and would touch.
Below me, the creek
marshes into loam,
disappears into the bay.

Feel the moss, stiff as goat hair,
soft as fur, yielding as sexflesh.
Strange as wing, gill, tongue.
I lie down between the stones,
my back and buttocks on gravel,
in the numbing water. Relax
like a corpse, a body, the rush
of the stream lifts me,

too embodied yet, but a little,
a little; I am washing down.

I lay my hair, my skull down
to my face, turn warmly numb.
Head pitched back against water
flow, my legs float free, ride.
What in the world do the trout,
*that* crow, make of this . . . thing
that the creek is washing down?
*Now* am I among the inhabitants?
Bouncing a little to keep my eyes
horizoned. Stretched and blue-white
like a saint or murdered prince
or lost, crazed thief. Homeward
bound, among the inhabitants, I
am quite literally freezing
my ass! Also, my head throbs.

And it *holds* me, it buoys and
floats me, like that red, big-
bellied, rusty-flanged barrel
floats and rings home, water-
borne

                    DONG    DONG . . .
          DONG.
                         lifts me to my feet.

     *

Or, face downed into the caverns
of roots, beneath the last tree:
work your fingers to the bone,
serpent-cock one on down, through
pine needles (stiffening) sharp,
dry-fanged, on down into pine-rot,
where the wet leaves break needles
back to soil, soil to sandstone,
sandstone to granite-rock, and

on down to lakewater, fish-gilled,
and a belly like the one swelled
you once came snuffling, hacking,
breathing-up out of, air-headed. . . .
Breathed, word-echoing, thighed.

*Hook that old yellow nail on down*
*until you rock-cradle, bone-bruise*
*your skull and cock and nipple*
*against the rock bottom:*
*clay to wood to limestone.*

When my fingers broke roots and
broken stone like gravel, I was
sucked in, clinched tighter
than hand-wrought nails
in seasoned wood, hardwood.
Split skin thrust into ground.
Childish memories bend and bleed,
heal like kid-scabs, house-silences.
Is that what home was? That silence?
Was it that hard? That ghost—
fleshly? I watch a wolf
or coyote or homeless hound
step into the moonlight, watch it
trust the night delicately, drink,
his manners exquisite,
or hers, being pure.

But I remember the wolverine
who hates man and kills hounds—
*Now watch, father, watch,*
*almost like that animal, almost,*
*your flesh and blood, your strange*
*kindred bone of bone, pitch headlong*
*like a fresh, clean, feather-rooted stone,*
*down into Furnace Harbor. Oh, no, no, no!*
*Naked, barely haired, she my daughter*
*sinking, her black hair twisting,*

*woven finally into weed and water,*
*coiled and ghosting it, turning,*
*her cheekbones laid bare, like*
*white roots, spreading—*
*and down, down, on down*
*she goes, beyond touching,*
*below the calls of father.*
*Delicate as snow, as paws,*
*her shoulders slick, nun-haired.*

\*

She and I sit
looking out over this
gray-green lake, this
inland sea, this soothed
colossus, this common belly,
singing, reciting, chanting
bits of songs we remember,
words, more often cadences—
familial, broken chants:
"O Wheel of Fortune, go
spinning around. . . . The
beautiful, Tennessee, waltz."
"There's a long, long road awinding."
"Hail to the victors valiant."
"Down by the Oh-hi-oh."
"It's nighty-night time for all
little babies, and you know who."
And she, fresh-fleshed, young-
thighed, returns into her woman's eyes.

Kindly, the bell buoy out-tongues,
outremembers us, measuring all children—

DONG     DONG     DONG

minding. . . .

Dead fathers,

                    dead daughters,
                    dead sons,
                    dead mothers
                    lifting and falling

in the numbed currents
of deadly fertile Superior:
down and drowned, rolling
forever with mouths open,
murmuring *wa-kay ka,*
*yay-wa-on we.*
                    Loosely:
We become ourselves
among the inhabitants
imagining births and deaths—
telling each other stories,
like those squirrels, or
those young men sandblasting
the restorations of
Furnace Harbor.

# VI

## THE LAND

*

Her cry is his cry, swallowed.
Shiftings of sand, maternal
veins of wound through stone.
Here, at Furnace Harbor, I hear us.
I hear her cry of inland waters, falling
into clear air, where the bell buoy
lifts and falls, ringing names
off the limestone headland. Now,
my ear of son, brother, father, echoes:

> through land, as a fetal heart is heard
> through water, through a woman's drummed
> inland waters, the earth's bloods fountain,
> pool and spread, gather and sow many-racial—
> navels, veins, tongues, wind aquiferous from
> the heart of oils, seep and filter, swell
> to deltas, under pressure, released to hammer
> thud, thud in the breast; as hooves come down
> valley and gap, slip, or along river floodplain,
> like our cleft selves, desperate to close,
> to hit, to ground ourselves, clenched, boned,
> horned, fleshed, sworded and cradled, all
> aquiform—flash like gods, flesh to stone;
> my mothers, who, where, were you? I
> hear where you came from, but did you
> hate your lovers, did you? I am all
> ear to ground down where we suffered
> the rumble of Algonquin winter sweep
> in the wine red face of the new American
> come to find and possess and claim you. . . .

Floated on the crust, spun above the core
of furnace, upon another kind or place
of ground zero, yet a kindred beat of heart
now more a twisting, a lifting, as upon water;
yet the old pressure, the same thunder of hooves
drum in the ear, the breast; on other
ground, in the Ohio Country, yet not home,
I sink into soil, shoulder and hip furrowed;

I measure, looking up, the rain forest sway
and rasp of corn fronds, Eden grown immense,
terrible, between earth and sky; measure
striations of greens more unearthly than
diving deep and deeper into the sea (for
these are light shot, light stricken, light. . . . )
these greens the spacey images of the earth's eye,
exposures of sun and ghost shadow—hair,
arm, hand, shoulder. . . . The corn-green
tides of this bottom land flooded with black
soot of mountains blown and burned and ground
into soil rich as freeze-dried blood
by the glacial seas, the continent winds
off an inland ocean of rock and lava
cold as ice. Fathering a birth is terrible.
The soil heaved, her head snapped back,
her throat pounded, her eyes all gone
into the light, the green, the blinding
shadows of . . . corn fronds, clouds, rain.
The field tips from under as we sway
and pitch over and over, to lie
upon the drifting buoyancy
of a spinning ark, going down.

Your eyes return. See me.
You rise, hull-hipped,
craft-buttocked, and
you roll away, you
walk, you kneel, you

       speak my name.

Rolling over, I mouth whatever the sky
drops on me, rolling over you:
Ear, a shell pressed to the ground,
hears all sounds together, coming:
as my Indian foremother heard the thud
of hooves resonant through clay:
heard them clear as day through

the pores of hollow trunks of trees,
or the moist, curled soil
gathered round the roots of trees,
the pores of her feet, her skin,
toes like tongues. . . .

*She heard them coming, like cattle bells.*
*They were soft in the distance, deadly.*
*But she waited in the woods, and she passed*
*her blood through them down to me.*
*Where her fingers etched the pine needles,*
*grooved them into V and V, nails and heels,*

> wide-eyed, twisting, tough-hide,
> hand's contour, curves, buttocks,
> brace and bend, the green
> stripped bough, plane and burr.
> The cunning-crafted gunwale—spine—
> palm cutting like a rudder, belly-downed,
> hands that arch, craft, hold—
> > building a ship, a fire,
> > unlimbering a fieldpiece;
> > making of a father, mother.
> Cold furnaces smoulder.
> Fire goes in and out.
> Shadows come, grow,
> disappear . . . man-shapes,
> shadows before or behind the fire
> come, go. Ghosts. Bodies.
> Fatal earth, earth-fatal.

> \*

We must begin again.
My eye begins again.
My ear's working again,
while others eye me:
who stalk like red ghosts
round the ironwork's
restoration:

The two women strip
near-naked, dive.
Slip through stone.
Their pale breasts
gleam.
The fur between
their legs
darkening,
crib-downed,
wakened, yet
sleeping.

I see the buoy first, and I
concentrate on its colors.
I see, watch it
rise and fall.
I focus my eyes on its
rise and fall, I
listen to its dull
cadences, ringing:

       DONG–DONG   DONG

            DONG

Now I can parse
the old beating,
old field rhythms,
magnetic fields
of force, drawn
breast to buttock,
socket-strung hips
furrow-rippled, lips,
jointed skull plates
that shift sea-bottomed,
skullbone of the earth's
crust, afloat
yet drowned, drift
of hand, swimming

fingers, reaching
down to catch the
deep place, moist,
where the worms go
thigh to thigh,
and hands clasp,
earth water-dance,
going down, round

eyes fast to feet,
hands tracing themselves
like webbed swimmers,
gestures hard remembering the
womb-beat, earththrust
fluid pound, pound,
land-membrane drummed
by skull fleshed spears spiraling
in the chambers of inland water,
the blood and spiralings
down bone to soft stone.
And the eyes rising, washed clean,
swinging like hips,
moving like fingers in the air,
the toes spreading, grip
the damp dirt, the
rain spattering all about,

closing the circle,
moving into
a whorl, a
dance of

bell-song,
rock and
water, fire
and tongue,
this dancing—
bell buoy tongued
to the bottom sand,

the rocks, the
sunken timbers,
submerged earth
of the northern
moon-lit, sun
curved, polar,
glacial, land.

The land is all
flesh, only that.
And bone, yes.
Flesh or bone
land, that dances
like we do, some
times, pounding
the one upon
the other, one
into the other:
afloat, embarked,
cargoed, mothered.

All her daughters,
all her sons,
all bloods, rise
and fall to rest
in Furnace Harbor.

# VII

## THE TIDES

*Second Strophe*

\*

Lift and fall,
neap, ebb, and flood,
tides even here, "where
the compass spins," inland,
where half a continent divides:
water, eyes, hands, rivers, spin,
close, and reach, grasp, draw.
Think of the tree bole, a whorling.
See the fires ringing a northern coast.
Look at your thumb, the palm's pincer.
Circle round another's eye. Currents
of river, the roots' home, the winds
and weather, vulvae, head and eye
of cock: all's a spinning sphere, a
sworl, circling, folding in and
opening out again. Tidal. Drawn.

Trust only what resembles the palms
of hands, the tones of voice that
sink down with the words in-folded
round each one, the voice
spiraling, rounding
silences into silence.
Trust that voice. And
all eyes that turn in-
ward, without dismay,
and then look outward,
but never away.

                    *

Tides even here,
where the land spins
magnetically, through copper
and iron and limestone,
round the lips of glacials,
shallow lakes with bottomless
holes, sources or outlets,
hand-scooped, shapen,
bass-headed, their finned

bottoms wavering, filling,
sinking, growing.
Like the lake that carried
me here, in my season.

*

Inland, the tides mark their shallow
hips in reeds, moss, rotting plank.
The fish move, moon-pressed, follow-
feeding, spawning, drifting — in
their dreaming, submarine way,
and suddenly move away, through
turned tides, where no tides are,
where currents chant mountain pressures,
the earth-headings of a magnetic bay:
water recalls its own way.

Glaciers even yet fill little holes
in Ohio, where pickerel rest, swell
beneath the sodden keel-board of
a half-sunken boat, its ribs
rotting into sea grass, muck-
bedded. And they rise and fall.
Perch, bass, muskellunge waver
round the yankee gunwales. And
the path to that lost mooring
in Newton Falls, or maybe Piqua,
or Chillicothe, Washington Court-
house, the buttock-lines of the
Ohio Country are marked in
roots, stumps in water,
winged and caged as the
loins that ghosted a way.
A stone age Indian fort
with rocks and stone, eight
feet high, hand-set, no
mortar, encases an earthern
fill a half-mile square

on a farm in southern Ohio.
The fort has a temple-ruin
at its midpoint. It's another
Furnace Harbor. And a mound,
or mounds, in Newark, Ohio,
form a great earthern womb,
and where the spring sun
at the solstice, the sexual
curve or arc, rhythm
of earth under sun,
comes through its fluted lips,
is a great, ground-sculpted falcon.
I knelt down to judge
earth-level the symmetry
of the falcon's wings—
two thousand years
afloat on the earth's crust:
both wings rose and fell
perfectly, softly curved!
It is the earth, over water,
that keeps these weights
and curvatures deep and true.
Cradles them, rightly ballasted,
each rock and stone and smooth
of earth, feeling hands knew.
Down the line of sight
from mouth of womb mound
to falcon, and beyond to
a cleft in the distant hills
behind me, a stout sapling
of maple stands placed
so precisely I cannot bear
to touch its pure and holy
coincidence of roots. How
could the chaos of seeds
and winds accomplish this
mythology of ourselves
more perfectly than we

can, clutched in sweat,
whimpering like children?
Mound, falcon, sapling,
cleft, remain cool as
courtesans, lunar.

*The sun is another tide.*
*The way it plumps and kills.*

        *

Here, at Furnace Harbor,
leaves circle down, swirl
like quicksand into black springs,
back behind the headwaters of the bay.
The sand curls back, whorls,
sucks your whole body out
into a stream running north
and south. It does not feel
like Florida undertow, or
Mexican riptide. This is a
subtler, wholer drift—
more persuasive, fatal.
The pull is infinitely gentle.
It embraces and urges, rocks.
It does not sweep and haul.
But, this tide is a mouth.
Its delta-suck is river-sourced,
with a long, slow river pull
behind it. Glacial. And it
flows into blood, through
veins of stone, in leaves.
It draws the earth round,
it hauls the star-sky, it
circles and swells the circle.
Northern, it turns your bones.
You hear it when you swim, and
cold, original cold, pulls your
hands down, creases the belly.
You hear it, too, hear it call,

this tidal, earthed, glacial
source and tongue and feel.

We kept the children
and the fool, restless hound
inside all that day, when the
bay felt itself to flood tide.
Superior was as fully calm as
a demented uncle at breakfast.
You could tell the earth had
come into a fatal point, whirling.
The sky was Mediterranean blue.
That night, we lay beside each other,
open-eyed, like astronauts,
hearing, or feeling (to tell the truth)
puma, coyote, bear, wolf, wolverine,
come forward, smell us, and sink
back into the heady, tidal night.
Heard and felt through the thin
skull-tissue at the temple. Where
the blood murmurs, veins answer.
A tidal rhythm down the sockets
of the spine. The hound knows, he
eyes storms fifty miles away.
His hairs, his back, stiffen.

He warns me
with a backward look, nose
tuned to what I can't hear.
Lying there, wrought beyond desire,
cock and nipples listen. All tides
rise and fall, here. Open and close.
Like pores, skull-seams.
As your bones, in fact,
breathe. Honeycombed, celled,
all tissues swell, relax.

Inland tides, where no

tides are.
       The bell buoy
                    poised
     to strike like snow
      flakes upon black
        water. . . .

# VIII

## THE FURNACES

*Third Movement*

\*

Men in matthew brady britches,
sack coats, hands on hearts, bedded
in rancid flannel, their navels
and wrists chafed red, rise
and rank here for their
regimental (company)
photograph.
                    Negative-skinned,
eyes like musket-bores, averted
but still staring at you, phosphorus-
ringed, sullen, they endure you.
In the booted fields and muck
of this place Furnace Harbor 1887
from Wisconsin, Iowa, Michigan,
money in their trousers, or socks,
or all spent and to win over again
betting for the Milwaukee whores kept
in the tent and circus concentration
camp outside Fayette. (Once, the boys
burned the stockade down and chased
the big-city promoters into the bay.
The girls broke loose and helped.
They drowned the vice-president of the corporation
in Big Bay du Noc. His brother, too.
But the boys still had to pay.
In fact, freed, the girls upped
the price. They used
a southern accent and called
themselves "niggah-honey" and
"swee-chile," and charged a surtax.)

Dusty-framed and filmed,
they stare back off the wall
through the brown ink of
Brady's cracked lens and
autograph. Ranked workmen
like the boys of the 3rd
Michigan at Manassas, or
"B" Battery, Wisconsin

Volunteers, before Pittsburgh
Landing: faces raw, un-
identified.

Flour-faced, their cheeks fishy
as badly cooked bacon,
their belt leathers looped, broken.
Farm boys, infantrymen with trousers
and mouths pulled tight, yet open.
Their cocks curled inside
canvas trousers, sunk red and white,
wrinkled as stale bait,
their limbs like turkey necks,
weathered pick-handles.
They file into the tent
every Saturday, lay down
their copper and silver,
step forward, drop
their drawers. . . .
                    Who burned
the goddamn place down?
It (the burning) was the
doom of Furnace Harbor.
They shot Sleet in the head
and they drowned his brother
black serge suit and all.
Had to hire a train from
Milwaukee to contraband
the girls back home again.

Their blank, wise eyes
bore into you, like all survivors.
They look and smell like
these old harnesses, stonesaws,
slag-rakes, canvas hats, boots,
a forged spike from the once-
famous railroad from Milwaukee,
Hemingway's boxcar, Crane's freighter.

Here's their lunch buckets, their
Bibles, their eyeglasses, wallets
water bottles, suspenders, their
iron pliers, pipe wrenches, lamps.

Charred edges of the portraits
of the men burned when the forge
blew up into the pines, or the
girls' oily tarpaulin went sky
high, or a lake vessel
leaking oil. Some of them
drowned funning in Big Bay
du Noc, while the headland
burned from lightning.
Some of their uncles or
brothers, and some of them,
were chopped into joints
along the breastworks
of Spotsylvania,
Cold Harbor.

                    *

I see faces rise here,
cheekbones red as fire—
they waver me down.
They sink or swim me home.
Mother, I'm afraid this is
another old death-song.
You birthed me to its tune
and you drowned yourself
in the Gulf of Mexico,
where you saved me once,
and once I saved you, but
not that last time, no,
you went on down, mother,
because you wanted to,
and this whole circling
that I call a poem is

anchored in you.
You have made me
        an old man, mother.

            *

In the "Hotel" they waken
to the sour-sweet stench
of bacon, sausage, side-pork,
the spatter and hiss of fry,
sourdough, eggs,

watch each other rise from bed,
careful of a man's privacy.
Quiet, speaking little and low.
Keeping their eyes down, watchful.
Then, the "free" meal, cramming.

Wakening, rising, the young men
twist their hips aside,
hiding their morning erections.
The older men rise wrinkled, shy
of loin, almost ashamed, not.

Moving in line to water, evacuate.
Then the company meat, black coffee,
and out into the sun again, near-blinded:
the bay-clear and blue-green morning,
the pines above the limestone headland

soughing in the light, early breeze
off Michigan, the lake rippling,
soft-grey horizon cloud-clearing,
the water in a lover's slapping
coming in, currents like glass

rock-veined, or old paned,
whorled and floral, fish-eyed.
They haul up their suspenders,
haul on their ironlike boots,

turn backs on the bay,
fire the furnaces,
break the pigs,
shovel slag.

\*

Pale ones made iron here, their
flanneled flesh red
       in the shadowed forests.
Red shadows, more black than red,
cast soft-blooded against
       tapestries of trees.
Luminous, black sky versus
       luminous, white boys
mirror, doubly fire-etched,
       the unearthly sexed: belly,
breast, thighs—negative-skinned.

The furnace-fire blossoming
       like lips, labia, wounds
rusted open, as the clayed bungs
gape here, petrified open. Flanges
caught on bent bolts
into the old brick
hearth, like a red
mine of mortar,
fallen, crumbling,
yet erect as an
Indian stone painting:
sooty towers, aimed sunwards.

When the sun strikes just so,
rust and brick, even the leaves
flame, fire blood-red as furnaces.
*November nights in Youngstown,*
*dank under acid rain, Negro*
*halfbacks blue-black,*
*ash-lipped in the Irish*
*Catholic cold, under*

*the burnt orange of furnaces,*
*sputtering arc lamps, molten*
*slagdumps and neon in Niles, Ohio.*
*The black halfback with bloody*
*nose and wide, white*
*eyes, shaking in the huddle.*
*I called his play again.*
*He came back with his white teeth*
*bloody, and I looked at that*
*damned sky, and called his*
*number again, and he wouldn't*
*cry. He wouldn't keep his head*
*down, either, going back in.*
*Three times, then crouched,*
*black and red face pressed*
*in the slaggy dead grass*
*end zone, weeping with*
*rage, fatherless, with*
*one pair of pants, among*
*the white boys, fists*
*raised, who were also*
*weeping but couldn't cry.*
*When he walked to the far end*
*of the bench, I looked at his eyes.*
*They were like agates, flint.*
*Men called millsoot in Youngstown*
*"black gold." Called him that, too.*
*Our real names were Constantino,*
*Triplett, Olzewski, Beach,*
*O'Connell, Pavlik, Del Bene.*

　　　　*

Here, the furnaces glow again.
I see them, like steel mills
burning the sky with gases.
Blood-red and brown, neither
salt nor sweet. Acrid,
a corrosive taste of chemicals

better left inert, buried
deep underground.

      *

The stoke-door swings open, falls
shut, clanging in the night
that comes down again,
rust-tongued, sullen
as Blacks or Polacks or Italians
in Cleveland, Pittsburgh.
From copper-hammering Toltec
down to the black and white man
hammering kiln doors open
at Furnace Harbor, or firing up
the open hearth at Republic Steel,
sledging, hot rodding, shoveling slag,
iron-and-steel is the sexless
Superman that made a myth of
one America, of Steel. The Toltec?
who only hammered copper into bowls?
And serpents of sacrificial knives, too!
Old Earth's vengeance for "Eden."

*And if you know where you're looking,
here, at Furnace Harbor, you will see
what this place was originally
and still is, northern,
where the bay goes clear
down, still as the mirror
on mother's dressing table,
bright as that kid's eyes
hammering limestone back
into restoration, hard
as the halfback's eyes.*

      *

At night, here,
fiery images of

kindred shoulders
man-borne: Italian,
German, Welsh, African,
Slav, at the untouchable
doors, the long iron pokes
that swing the gates upon the blast
of iron all natural to fire,
a lava two thousand times hotter
than any rock or stone could bear.
Here, they piddled and puddled iron,
but they burned to it, sure
as the swaying cauldron womb
of skyrocketing, cold steel showered,
meteor-mothered, comet-cocked;
their nativities of flesh
glisten red in the furnaces,
blistering, blackening each one
in the melting pot of mid-
America, that is no metaphor.

The ironmen are all our fathers,
old mothers, rank as bacon,
chaste as the hulls of white-
planked lake schooners
that brought the owners in
serge, the auditors, creditors,
the chairmen of the board.
How the sleek buttocked, proudly
cut prow of the schooner
rocked at complacent anchor
there, in that brilliant bay,
her spars and furled sails
like the limbs of an angel!

And they lined up the ironmen
like the shoddy cannon-fodder
they were, and filmed them forever.
Even the red-breasted, unearthly
glow of slag, of steel, of neon

that washed the pale bodies downed
or erect, in the hasty bedrooms
of Chicago, Detroit, Youngstown,
even those comet-tails of the
Saint Teresas of the lakeskies,
Catholic Puritan bleeding Christ
of the steelsky, immortalizing the mechanized
seasons of millwound and fleshfruit,
was denied: O the romance of Steel!
Now the pale, shining gulls
tilt crosswinged in the Michigan sky,
red hawks plunge like murderous convicts
through the black interstices of pine and pine,
out upon the serenely rippling bay, where
the buoy, faint in the distance,
chimes. . . .

*where a lakeboat sails,*
*gentle palms laid lightly*
*across her tiller, her*
*timbers held in sway, her*
*joints opening, closing,*
*swelling and relaxing,*
*taking tide and currents,*
*wind-direction, wet-thumbed,*
*sobering, sailing her*
*on through, past*
*Furnace Harbor*
*west heading,*
*into another*
*furnace . . .*

where, transfigured,
the gull turns
into Arctic Tern
centering, then
reversing the circle,
as a hound will double back,
retracing the scent of his going,

turn and disappear again, wheeling
nose-down, his tail high and flagging
yet another circle, opening back out,
tongue-flying, eyes dark with spoor
and the sunlight in the night air.
And his earth-smelling fur
reeks of tides steaming
on the earth of fires. . . .

So those, too, who fly,
sail, track, or mine . . .
curling back, rounding
home here into Furnace
Harbor, where fire
damasks the forest,
velvet as flushed
thighs, open as
vulvae black-haired,
flash-fleshed,
open-hearthed. . . .

*where the big-bellied*
*buoy rests and rocks,*
*pivoting the very point*
*of intersections,*
*sex and geology,*
*iron, stone, flesh:*
*bolt-blooded,*
*earth-skinned:*

\*

Charcoal and limestone,
ore, air, fire
blasts the acid gases
up the furnace, while
the slag, like glass,
sinks, and the iron
seeps down, like blood.

Slag and iron, molten,
pool in the bay of the hearth,
layer there, like oil, water,
drawn or tapped out
two holes, clay-bunged.

So, the buoy's belly is natural,
too, as tools and humans, and
stone, bronze, copper,
iron. From the beginning
the earth is chemical, mineral,
and so is man. And fire.
Furnace Harbor is one core.

The white man seems drawn to the cores
of the earth; the red Indian content
with the surfaces, land or sky.
The white man stares deeply, deeply
into the fire, while the woman
cooks supper, in an iron spider.

      *

A stooping, raw-fleshed,
knob-boned man draws the clay plug,
opens the furnace
              in the night, his
           head a black-blot
        nimbused with fire.
           All his sinews start.

Like the trees, he burns bright as resin.
The bay, like a sister, stays clear
as glass and takes it all in:
her spasm-riddled brother,
man-shape with the
preternaturally
long arms.
           All his ore dis-
appears into the cold, burning sky.

Swallowed into the night sky,
starlit as Eden's fallen sky,
blood-red in the furnace peephole.
He leans and peers in. I see his face
blazing in the light of that fire-hole—
nose, forehead, cheek, lips, teeth . . .
and then:
nothing,
nothing.

        Gone.
           Ash-gone,
                into the dark,
                      into oblivion,
                          the core.

                  O

    *

Magnetic north
pulls us back
into Furnace Harbor.
I am drawn limb-downed
into this, as though my
cock were the itchy meat of
a drifting, half-burnt pine log.
Building a fire,
scrambling eggs.
Gathering chips.
Relieving myself,
that shake and
bone-shudder.

    *

*A canoe yawing*
      *with each stroke.*
*I keep bending it back,*
      *it keeps yawing*
*like an arrow. . . .*
      *I bend, listening,*

*I put the paddle up,*
          *lay it athwart the gunwales,*
*let the bow swing, falling off,*
          *my fingers trailing in lakewater,*

*as on land, fingers sink curving*
          *beneath the stone into leaves*
*and down into loam, warm-cold,*
          *where hands grow still, lipped*
*in the wombed hearth of a*
          *maiden who was once a lover,*
*in the lakewaters of innocence*
          *imagination cannot recover.*

          \*

Easy, tanned, the young men drift
their skinned hands about the
ironwork's restoration.

Already, boy-man,
your picture hangs
not without features,
on the charred wall
of that old Michigan
ironworks museum.

Tonight, the cries
of those ironsodden
furnacemen echo
mute as bones
through our low voices,
quiet around a cookfire.
Still, we are ringed with fire,
the invisible stars, passion's core,
so deeply burnt. Ash
to ash, mother-spent,
father-killed, serpent
tongued. Blooded.
Impure as iron.

*

Across the bay
the cries return
full-throated, sub-
marine,          chanting:
*cry of gull and wolverine,*
*of man and woman locked*
*beneath the evergreen,*
*their knees and carven*
*toes, their sweet nails*
*clinging, their bellies*
*dripping gum, their*
*openings coupled in*
*secret, night circlings,*
*the night's black tree-*
*dance on the ground*
*of their furnaces,*
*secret in pine-cover,*
*in the fire-dance*
*of Furnace Harbor.*

*

On their way home,
the two Indians
watch demons drowning,
coiling like nosebleed
down the hearth-lit
furnaced circles
down the night-shore . . .
seeing, witnessing,
the burning torsos of
iron and limestone
flamed shadows,
black-smouldering
flesh phantoms
eyeball to eyeball,
tree to tree, glow-
ing hair-fires in

the pines and offices
of Furnace Harbor.

*Tell: Dong-dong*
> *to make the channel,*
> *ironmen to Indian*
> *burial. We womb,*
> *die, flame and shall*
> *rise again: wet*
> *with love,*
> *with the sweats*
> *of birth cold as*
> *birth — yet burning:*

*Demon-fires.*
*Stone-fires.*
*Lake-fires.*

The Indians gape,
> open-mouthed,
> > slack-jawed
> as motoring tourists
in Struthers, Ohio, are
> stunned at the maws
> of the open hearths, thunderous
seas of steel showering, molten.
> > The asphalt street a black nightmare
> > through a tunnel of flames. . . .

They hold on, swaying
> in their new canoe,
> now equipped with an Evinrude.

*"Hayzoos J.! You see that?"*
*"Yeah, that's french-fuckin mumbo-jumbo, man."*

> > And they paddle on
> out of sight.
> > On down the southern sweep

of Michigan, rednesses of sun,
fire, paint, wine, red-rimmed
eyes, thighs (one of them is
menstruating) amid visions

visions! of the demon-fires in the pinedark,
a bay like grandmother's longhouse, the ribbed,
pliant breasts of that Anglican girlchild
they hauled out of Lake Fanny Hoo with flesh
like split hickory, nipples like
gooseberries, and pigmentation
of Cheyenne warrior erections.
"Jes keep paddlin, Methodis-ass,
and we maght make it. . . . "
The lift and suck
ride their Indin
asses home, virgin.
Floating feathers?
Drowned? They
made it.

                    *

*In the agate center of a pane*
*of handmade glass the eye whorls*
*outwards from inward all directions.*
*The thumb-knot in the middle*
*twists and turns: your geo-*
*graphy is how you were born.*
*You spin it back again, and*
*tug on a navel-cable, like*
*the bell buoy in*
*Furnace Harbor.*

Furnace-mouthed,
reflecting fire
like the ripples
of a flat stone
sent skipping
into black water,

steaming from my
cookfire, husbanding,
humming in the pines

like shrapnel, iron
in the sinking heart-
sockets of a father,
the love like molten
water, eyes like loam:
fingers of limestone:
not able to say anything.
Not possessing the right
to say "I made you."
Because he didn't.
She did. Knowing,
not knowing who she
birthed, doomed.

       *

Here, look here, hold
the stone like this,
flip your wrist, flat,
see? and the damned thing
will skip five times
before it sinks
into Furnace Harbor.

Iron whirls and whangs.
Iron maidens railroaded
in from Milwaukee, let
loose upon these ironmen.
Finn, fraulein, colleen:

she finds her shape
in the furnace flame.
She slips her fingers
beneath the bone, lifts
her eyes, hears the buoy.

She watches, remembering,
a long, pale back bend.
She has guided a longship,
disappearing, going down.
She turns back, homing.

The insides of her thighs
are webbed with blood, a
thumbprint's whorl.
He is silent, weeping.
She is quietly. . . .

       *

Daddy, with visored cap and slung camera.
Mother, broad-beamed in bell-bottoms, and
two T-shirted kids, YMCA across their ribs,
sit fishing from a dock nobody dreams of
rebuilding. Dangling lines that will never
reach bottom, never tempt that hole they
don't even know they are fishing into,
and for all their expensive, live bait,
they better hope they never reach into,
never hook that kindred thing there
and have to drag it off the bottom,
unhook, with trembling fingers. They
would have to batter it to pulp first,
and even then it would quiver and stare.
The man is tough on the line,
jerking and hauling, heaving
the bait about, throws it out
about eight hundred feet,
and furiously winds it in.
He's an auto worker from Pontiac.
His uncle is a steward in River Rouge.
His father is a retired foreman
now residing in Milwaukee.

After ten or fifteen minutes of this
weekend safari, the lines are abruptly

reeled in, fast as restroom masturbation.
With much chattering, curses, they
pack up and move on, like chickens.
"Nothing here. Shit, no fucking fish!
Nothing to see. Piss on it, let's go!"
Bundle their screaming kids into the
air-conditioned camper and move on.
You can hear them five miles
down the road.

                    *

Behind that furnace,
behind that broken tower right over there,
the one I just pissed behind when
nobody was looking, two negatives
broke their hands open against
each other's cheekbones, in August,
1875. Maybe it was June, sultry.
They split each other's face wet.
Flesh slits open, mouths so quick
you can't see it happen, just hear
the sodden hit—skin frozen white
just before the blood comes welling.
Then it streams, deltas all down
a boy's or a man's face.

Flesh pinched tight between bone and bone
splits like magic. A face runs red,
wide open. Ragged tears. Sometime,
you should see a man's face
opened, saliva, blood, tears,
dripping off his thin chin,
his lips tight but trembling,
and sick, all of a sudden.

It's a lesson, all right.
Lesson in origins, iron.
Turf, bed, pride.
Our furnace of fluids,

terrible as Heaven's dry.
Here's a face, blood-red,
                    dripping. . . .

           *

Sleeping in rancid flannel,
working day after day in the sun,
on the hot planks, the rails, facing the furnaces,
and night after night in the stacked bunks
so narrow you have to embrace yourself,
never wholly naked, never entirely clean,
without women, breathing each other,
cutting, hauling, stacking, burning—
after too goddamn much useless doing,
too much gassy, mocking yap,
too much greasy bacon, they
came together like animals.
They lined up in the tent
and stripped and pounded
their punk out like whales.
But finally, they fought.
They fought like men,
missing the cold, yellow eye,
the whiplike calm, the fatal
steadiness of cat, wolf,
wolverine. They wept.
With rage. Children.
Attack, fire, burn, hate—
white men in the Wilderness.

           *

Therefore, still, implacably,
Indians peer down from their
presences, here, among the pines.
Dark and cool, with cold blood
in their eyes. And the walls of
limestone swell above the glistening,
clear bay. The night-bellied bell buoy

rings and rings, and not in benediction.
It is chanting, it is urging the blood on,
lake-black-magic, terrible to the white man,
of tidal seas of semen coiling
like albumen back into his eyes.
The buoy DONG–DONGs your brain,
and echoes, echoes, in the core.

There is laughter coming
across the lakes, and dim
outlines offshore, just
outside the fire's glow:
A drunken greeting hails:
        "Goo-baa."
                And we hear
paddles clump lengthwise across
birch gunwales wrapped in hide.
I am half-awake, buried in sand,
sheltered beneath the fallen timbers.
Downshore, a point of orange flame
dims and flares in the lake-fogs.
A figure moves across its own light.
Ironman, or Indian, or murdering
fisherman, or woman wandering late?
All, and dangerous. Ghost-flesh,
human. In the moonlight, I

look down into the bay at Furnace Harbor.
I see a ghost-face rising to meet me there.
Calm, wavering yet steady, its lips
opening and closing,
yet at rest, smiling:
it greets me like a
lost brother, sister.

      *

Nothing can be restored here,
because nothing was ever lost.

What *was* here is gone.
Dead, buried, forever.
Just as we are, living.

So these shadows,
                    human, furnaced, treed:
the meaning of the poem,
the whole place fills me, utterly
comprehensible, the distant cries
in the shadows, old mouths
mouthing the ancient layerings
of needles, stone, kilns . . .
the buoy rings constantly
a constant measure
                    of rapt, taut thighs
on the ground, relaxing,
tightening of sinew,
                    melting of bone,
                         making mind of

my birthing, which is a
dying back and a thrusting on

into Furnace Harbor, which
does not exist,
is nothing, is
and was a stage,
a film, a medium
of eye and mind and hand,
of the terrific spectacle
of cell and element,
of memory that does not
exist, of time which
we imagine, of relics
of which the bell buoy
only remains: mute,
mechanical, serene.

# IX

## THE BUOY

*Third Strophe*

\*

Smoke rises through Indian suppers,
drifts through the gray, green pines.
In the late evening, when trees and cliffs,
even the rollers coming in, coil, recoil,
then flare as a demon painting on velvet,
the bay shimmers in the long sun,
shadows recreate themselves, then fade,
and dogs echo
   across the deep
     clear bay.
       And the rusty bell buoy
         rings in the wave's fetch.


        Dong Dong
        Dong Dong


              Dong. . . .


   *

Off Furnace Harbor, off
the headland of smouldering pines
and the granite and limestone
cliffs, Superior in its guises
of lakes and oceans and rivers,
whispers in. It is not
the thunder I hear, in Ohio,
nor the swell of foothills
nor the slopes of the Appalachians
I see move in this autumn,
this stillness of havoc, this
whorl of seasons, this mare
with the auburn shine of
centuries of deserts, stallion-flung,
or the fine-boned and nostriled
passion of mountain
brooks she hastens to in her
matings, wondrous-eyed, trembling-flanked.
Tonight, a wolverine, a deer, a hound,
sinks down in solitude to drink.

Superior abides all that, that fur. But
it waits, upon gravity.

                *

A sleek-hulled, polished cruiser
from Milwaukee, Green Bay, or Duluth,
her twin Chryslers purring in oil,
ghosts into berth at Furnace Harbor;
its white-ducked master never so sure,
as alien, as the lines he casts into the bay.
Switches turned on and off: passageway, galley,
electric compass, depth-finder.
The languid girl in the white bikini,
brown and fully-grained
as the mahogany decking,
balances a martini in her bows,
while "Roy's Toy" (Duluth),
arch and remote as the girl,
closes her beam to a decrepit dock.
Smoked glass and explosive
bubbles aft enrichen
a perfect afternoon, perfectly
locked into Furnace Harbor.
Cockpit illumined,
Roy's face momentarily
fades, grave and stern.

                *

There are faces, eyes, wavering
here, girl, beneath yours.
Beneath your hardnesses, in furnaces
and cheap canoes, buoy and bay.
I see you know that, too,
in your knowing eyes, plain
as that knowing cross of yours
of thigh to thigh, drawn from
some loined or naveled memory
beyond your saying. But here,
the water like glass, the

curling of your hairs
upon a bell's tolling rings
deeper than you hear, their
ragged musketry.

Are you secretly
(secretly!) pregnant already?
Where is your Daddy? Does
your Momma know?

This buoy revolves its
soft underbelly, too,
mossed into its rise and fall.
And the hair between your legs
will grow gray, deciduously.
Now, your belly lifts, falls
in the running lights, marking its time,
rippling when you rise, sinking
into caverned sand bottom
when you lie back, sink down.
Bleached, your nether hairs
dry, curl, pine-bushed.

                    *

This bay signals another kind of pregnancy:
clean, white hull locked tight in a frozen bay,
the fishing family, these barren men, will stay
until the trees and tides freeze hard again as lime
and all this, restored, burns a second time.

All caught, frozen here, striking poses,
the pawky, stone-faced poses
of a Brady.
                    The buoy is
lifted, and it falls, dong-dong,
to sound the channel,
to raise in mist smoke signals
from Ironmen to Indian burials.

The iron is raised, the old men
call, sundown like salt wine
cast upon the limestone shingle:

old milk, old sperm in urine smell
sunk in the board rot of this old hotel:

Their canvas pants, their spectacles, nailed
upright to the sootstained museum wall.

# X

## THE DOCK

*Recursé*

\*

$B$ack along the curve of shoreline from the headland
where the two women and my daughter who is wound
in a flannel blanket and hunches black-eyed, blue-lipped
like a survivor before the driftwood fire—the women
now seaman-sweatered, heavy-ribbed, and defined
in the afternoon grayness that lifts so suddenly out of the land
on these shores where the sealight, shallow at noon, flows
into the air, is swallowed and the continent is ocean
and gray and darkening like my daughter's plunge, her
descent into the truth of herself and her parents and friends—

I pick my way back along the curve of shoreline from the headland
where the women stand alongside the shuddering child and stare
out to sea, because women have always feared and loathed the sea
for the white-bellied men who will not farm, nor cut trees,
nor tend cattle or horses or sheep or any warm-blooded thing
but must go off into the darkness of the earth, into the darkness
of the sea, the great lake colder and more merciless even
than the ocean, to prove as sailors, like miners, that they
were never birthed, never suckled on warm milk, and so
cannot die because in their sky-echoing conceptions
they are already dead and boned and socketed and white,

I pick a way—who am yet boyish in my love of water,
my love of women, torn between the blood and milk warmth
and the ghastliness of an ocean of fresh water that, so
cold, holds no life whatever, so there is no beach, no sand,
and even the ships that sail upon it, newly keeled, look
like relics and ribbed specters, their irons and seams sunken
already as they come down the ways and momentarily float—

over the granite, limestone, sandstone rocks and bones of
continental shelf where no crustacean life eons old mills,
over the undermined timber and roots and branches of the forest
sea-sloshed, twisted, strewn, polished gray, to a Michigan dock
itself an artifact, instant antique, not seriously intended to be
lasting or believable or even momentarily useful, a kind of
gesture or grimace or joke of a dock, so typically, fatally
northern that, wind and winter storm stripped, bolted, nailed,

water-piped and crosshatched in its own accumulations of despair,
in a gradual hysteria of reproduction or restoration or history,
the dock kind of hangs there, like a jilted bridge.

      \*

Out beyond the pier, in the mouth of the bay, beyond any stretch
of imagination, rocks the buoy, the fact,
the artifact beyond art, the enigma.
Lugged to the bottom (how!), it girdles, rolls, tips its
incessant, unvoiced tongue

Dong-Dong

Dong

Dong-Dong-Dong

Whatever in the world it is, or was compounded of, was intended for,
or might have served in whatever capacities, it is
none of them now. It is the dock's impossible landfall,
the point missing its line or circle, fixed point beyond a fix,
neither savage nor mechanical, neither strange nor known.
Smoke rises from Indian fires through the pines,
drifts out to where the buoy blows it away.
There is, what we are not enabled to see.

      \*

Impossibly—inconceivably—
past the buoy, her bows fleshed white
as the loins in a flash of mother,
"Roy's Toy" bends into the bay, to the
dock, her wake without even the illusion
of ghosts, so chaste and isolate.
Her twin Chryslers reverse like sinking jugs.
Teak, her brightwork like ivory, her glass
tinted smoke, the yacht backs way, comes
to dock, and a pale figure casts me
a line. She's secured into Furnace Harbor,
as night falls; landfall, and a berth:
out of Duluth, clean-hulled still,

her naked bows glow like those white
plastic jesuses. The mighty Roy, grave and brown,
switches off depth-finder, stern lights,
console, gangway, and leaves one on
in the galley. Goodnight, Roy, you don't
know it yet, but you'll never waken from
this night's dream of rolling, pitching women.
This night in Furnace Harbor will give you a
morning and empty you for the rest of your life.
This is your Cemetery Hill, buddy, and no shrink
will ever be able to explain why from this night
forward you will imagine nothing more to desire.
You, the boat, and the girl will become
what you were—memorial images
of desire. Sunken in Furnace
Harbor. Buoy-donged down.
Star-watered, furnace-flung,
fire-found, and lost illusion,
all victory gone.

                    *

Roy on the advice of his shrink will consider
his demise, his loss of real interest in anything
including sex, business, golf, boats, politics,
due to, variously, his middle age, his
mother's asceticism, his sneaking suspicion
(imagined) that he was queer, the natural
letdown following the sexcruise
dreamed of and plotted since age eight,
his despair following an out-and-out brawl
during which his wife's adopted daughter, age
sixteen, not only destroyed in stand-up, fair
fight both his sons, aged seventeen and
twenty-four, but as well his:
three-car garage, sauna, patio self-
cleaning grill, the patio itself, the private
putting green, the Pontiac Firebird, the
VCR plus its giant, life-sized screen, *and*
his devoted bird dog Angel Lips,

his hybrid rose and marijuana-
orchid crop along with its
multiseason, circum-uniflex sound and
video conservatory greenhouse over whose
audio system the bedrooms of the sixteen
neighboring houses were not only bugged but
videotaped, and whose plexiglass cuneiform
panels were in direct technological descent
from the nose and turrets and cockpit
bubbles of the only things he ever loved
in his entire life (excluding his Aunt
Mamie): Mitchell and Flying Fortress bombers
and Mustang and Thunderbolt fighters.
But he and his shrink will be wrong,
wrong, and wrong again, over two hundred
and twenty-one times wrong, in actual
count, in succession, over a period of
three years, two and one-half
months analysis and cross-examination and
soul-searching complete with confessions,
revelations, religious conversions,
and two volumes of industrial biography —
the shrink was wrong,
I repeat, it was all the fault of
Furnace Harbor, of that afternoon he
steamed prow-up into the Presences
of bay and Furnace and Ironmen.
We recall his face upon anchoring
(that maneuver, too, hilarious!)
was already grave and stern. . . .
That evening, over Calabash and Scotch,
he said to the young woman,
"Has it ever occurred to you
that you *are* my great-grandmother?
On my father's side? And that I
am the grandmother of myself?"
He was quite serious. More so,
when she said she'd known that

the third time they'd made love
parked beside that funny-feeling cliff:

*they'd kept drifting in, only the anchor*
*was fast. And the boat rocked all*
*night, but the lake was like glass.*
*"I wish we'd gone to Chicago, like we*
*planned," she said. Later, to his shrink,*
*Roy would characteristically counterattack:*
*it was the mere fact that he*
*passed that goddamned buoy and*
*cruised old "Roy's Toy" into that*
*goddamned weird harbor in the first*
*place. "Have you ever* been *in the twilight zone,*
*goddamnit? I don't mean just watched*
*the goddamn thing, but sailed right*
*fucking damn* into *it? Then shut to*
*hell up!" He was right, sort of.*

   *

In Ohio there are Indian burial mounds
that are not as perilous as Furnace Harbor,
only sneakier. But for Roy, and the girl, this bay
and that invisible, dong-donging buoy were enough.
Roy has steamed into the enigma of *himself,* and of *her,*
and of words all images, memories that toll and tell
themselves alone in the catacombs of
skulls and hips and bones
flesh-furred, belly-tongued
like furnace mouths, mineral-sexed
amid the passages of trees, and limestone
all water-wrung, raised upon earth
as the burial mounds—serpent and womb—
drift down Ohio, borne like chronicles.

And now, upon the harbor and the headland
where the firelight flickers like knowledge,
the Indians peer over in their presences.

And I knew finally that they were real.
They alone, in their shrouded, pine-struck
shadows and voiceless tongues, proved true,
sounded-in by the buoy to this hanging dock.
And the boat, shining thing
of the crafty, is traitorous,
its skewed bows, its freeboard
sleek to its mathematical curve,
its cunning equation of mass
and displacement and ballast,
lifts and falls on her lines,
in the gathering darkness, turns
Indian, turns fluid, turns again
into atmosphere, into milky haunt.
And crafty, the human eyeglint
turns to chalk, sand, limestone.
What I perceive remains trans-
parental, but perception itself
coils out and is gone, forever, into
the absolute nothing
of the absolute thing,
like a line lost overboard,
its bitter end left unsecured,
and it coils once, twice,
and seasnakes down.
And the Indians move
round and round
their perfect fires,
obsidian-eyed,
looking down.

May my daughter, and
her mother, and the daughter
milky in her womb, and
our friend, not wander
one inch beyond the illusion
of our bright fire, because
this is a terrible, desperate place, I think,
this Furnace Harbor, this dark and starlit,

eyeless pitch of the earth's ledge,
this rocking verge, this seaskinned skull.

*

*And this, too:* last night
within range of headlong flight
from this . . . a place, is it?
I was a father, again.
Of, again, a daughter.
Of the mother, again
mother of a daughter
known already, already named
though not yet a full day fled
to womb and home, from the
snake and vaults of her terrible,
pathetic navigations and her
lost brothers', sisters', those
alkaloid brightnesses in darkness,
or vice versa, of the saltwort,
the plantash, of the limestoned
babylon of sacrificed priests.
Viper-headed, gigantic-tailed,
the mirror-eyed mariners

of the stone groin, drowned by
the shiploads, like desert legions,
and one, one last helmsman, lover,
makes it to the magic grotto,
the fatal parlor of repercussion.

Rudders right in: wump, or wang,
hits. Belly flops. Kiss. Whatever.
And otherworldly, the oceanic
concussion: gong.

Or, a kindly and homey
greeting, is there, as here,
in her lowest tone? "I'm
pregnant again, I was apparently

born to have daughters
and know each one instantly

when I roll over. Where's
the car? We're leaving."

       \*

Now, another voice, the
girl on the "Toy's" bow
addresses me. Low, hushed, she says
"Did you get the line? What the hell's
that ringing? It must be my head!"
"It's the buoy," I say, "at the entrance
to the harbor. What line?"
"Oh. Jesus! I didn't hear it, coming in.
Do you own this place?"

       \*

In the mountains, in Mexico,
There is light, incredible color,
and then there is night,
darkness total, unfathomable.
In Mexico, mortality is sharp like that.
First the terrible sun, then . . . out.
At the fall of light, even the
parrots shut up. The sky falls.
Brazier-shadowed, the stone walls
of church and fortification rise
to hold back what descends, comes
upon village and valley and city.
There remains flickering a pulse
upon the land. Like blood, yes.

Upon the ocean, or even beside the sea,
the globe's darkness—the world's arch—
is never complete. Morning remains,
lightfall stays a human bit, visible,
waiting, the curve holds true, darkness
rests upon the planetary thing.

On the darkest night, the sea shines,
and all is a process, a continuation,
edge and closure like a turning blade,
a shaft of metal, though plunged, still
bright as brain and eye to all
who sail the sea in memories
of the world's full, round image.
Bless the ocean and those men
and women and children and those
aged and weakened who yet may
live upon it, suffer its deaths,
its hilarious, irresistible plungings.

But at the domed, concentric curve of
Superior's wombed and locked placidity,
upon its plummeting, polar sky,
the land at night, *and* the waters,
disappear entirely. Fathomless, lightless,
the earth's lake rises into the sky
and resumes the darkness of Chaos,
and all *in* it, is this invisible shining,
shining, that comes not from stars, or
firelights, or memories, or ganglia.
From the snow cap? From the poles?
It shines in the eyes of mad Indians,
In the innermost veins of stone,
within the roots buried, like shafts,
within the wrathful chambers of the wolverine,
that hates mankind more than life.
I imagine, I imagine at the last void,
there's not earth, not time, not space,
but inland sea, all cold and pure as Superior.
Find at last, here, the end of words,
whatever the brain might recall
in its first hour, what the eyes
can tell their tongues to sound.
That the morning, here, at Furnace Harbor
should lead to this, for all its
bright and sexual fantasies of richness!

Of the world's miraculous changes, and
of words, fantastic as stories!

To stand before this . . . oblivion:
imagine being forced—your face—down inside
the long grooved curve of a root,
the flesh and bone of your face and skull
shed, stripped, as you shove
your head on through, down
to the water drop at the tip
of the tap root, and there,
all weeping whiteness of
eyeball, you stare
yolked and boned-headed
into the waters of the womb
of the world. Where you
came from. Where the buoy
is lugged rocking at the
bottom. Then where is night?
Where is day? You feel
your mind twist and slack
with the tidal swells—

      Dong-dong. Dong.

         To groove the channel,
         from Ironmen to Indian
         burial. . . .

   *

                In all his imaginings,
his silences, was this what Roy desired, dreamed
(No. Wait. Wait. Roy yearns)
of fief, kingdom, harem, home, happiness?
Who knows, but it was not what the Indians
who sailed and painted and homed desired,
for they knew all too well they had already
lost it, so settled in a kind of dog-grinning
defiance for what they could. Not Roy.

Perhaps Roy dreamed of Paradise.
Perhaps, deeper yet, Roy desired atonement,
some version of pastoral, or permanence or
annunciation, like a bourgeois Macbeth.
Like Indian-weary Custer,
Roy thought to hell with it and quit.
Long remembered, longer endured, the gongs
or dongs of the harbor buoy will do that,
did that incrementally, ineluctably, to Roy.
Later, following his canonization, he was wont
to repeat his favorite profundity: "I fear
dying, I do not fear Death; love is fear.
I forget, if I ever knew, what death is, but
it is not fear. Perhaps, perhaps, death is Love."
He shambles, he weeps, he chants:
breaks into song in the faces of
wind, treads crying with terrible
joys the intestinal fortitudes
of Rhode Island's fallopian
coasts. In the throes of
Roy's uttered abandon
he renounces and reigns,
a ghastly hymn of himself.

Dong. Dong-dong.

And he names the million gulls
that or who flocked to his mind.
Arranges the billion sailing boats
from Manhattan to San Luis Obispo
into patterns, formations, squadrons
that ten years after his death
transfigure college football
forever. The triple-winged, slant
doubled-back "V" in singular
motion "T," with convoluting
flankers and the famous anchor-
to-the-wind shift, called "angel-lipped,"
has since become the normal

alignment in the third and three
situation, but only outside the twenty
in the closing terrible seconds
of the third quarter.
Roy desired immortality
thus, and he got it.
Ding-ding of reality
ping-ponged Roy
to his tomb, notorious
at last.

We pray, so
long, buenos
noches, guy,
nice
going.

                    *

But wait! Roy's soliloquy:

"Twenty sea miles today
at three knots per hour
with no will, no desire
to go any faster, go at all.
Just sat at the bridge, staring.
Did the 72° right turn into
this weird bay, so awful quiet.

Hell, all my big ideas . . . fantasies.
Sunk back down to dreams.
And now I can't even sleep.
They rise, each by each, like memories.
Shit! Like each duck me and
Angel Lips . . . hardly a ripple!
She never broke the skin. . . .

This girl, now. What in the world
am I gonna do . . . God damned
buoy, I wish to god that friggen

bell would sink or rust shut.
Jesus-Christ-on-a-coaster,
I think maybe I'm already dead.

Gotta get some sleep. That port magneto's
going. Maybe all we ever wanted was
to die? Open my eyes—can't see nothing!
Damn boat's a dream, a fantasy, too.
Where's the sense in it, I ask you.
Damn port magneto . . . they *guaranteed* me!"

   *

Odd, now I think of it, how our chief
words clot their vowels against consonants
themselves inchoate, murky, darkened:
"Fuck," "Love," "Dead," "Womb."
These are our home utterances, like "Run."
How bright the word "fire," and somber are
"daughter," "woman," "father," "man."
The words of *man* sound their meanings
better than we can. Combine, then,
these:

   *From the dock, I see the fires*
  *of Indian suppers drift like fog*
  *across the harbor and the silent,*
  *rocking yacht where the girl*
  *lies locked in the arms of the*
  *drifting mother's son who brought her/him*
  *at nightfall into Furnace Harbor.*
  *May the whites of her eyes not show*
  *full wide in the knowledge of their birthing.*

   *From the dock, the shadows of the*
  *sunken ship, the lost creeks, the burnt*
  *trees, root and rock clench like feathers,*
  *arch and recede.*

   *From the dock, I see smoke*

*from Indian supperfires, banked
yet bright, drift like voices
through the pines, behind the
furnaces, where their figures
move, more than ever now a
dance of the doomed.
The night mists, shapes follow
and shift like grandparents. . . .
What a gracious fragility rings
and closes us here, as evening
dissolves into Furnace Harbor!
Even the buoy is silent, rocking
like a grandmother, her deep-veined
hands clasped upon her thighs.*

\*

The harbor grows deep and clear enough
to swallow each of these: flesh, stone,
voices, fire, green off the headland;
and the wind's steady at twelve knots,
from north-northwest,
rippling up the bay. . . .
All is right, this way,
this moment, image
and memory, moving . . .

moving to lonely men who twist and burn,
wet in woolen blankets, stiff and growing
old, hands on hearts, at
their regiment's commemoration,
by "Matthew Brady,"
before Antietam. . . .

\*

Off beyond the restoration,
suppering Indians talk rabbit.
The old warriors are well blanketed.
All the violences of the heart
burn down as the wind shifts

and falls, softer than flesh,
darker than hands at night
that shine and fade at last
among all their possessions.

And the roots, the stones,
ember-shift, water-hipped.
And one other turn is done.
One last word, is there?
And now, the buoy's one
dong, or gong, one only.

We are simply
all going down
into earth, and
sailor, on down
to death, yes,
watery, and shining,
shining, like eyes
in memory.

        *

And now, from the yacht parked
beside the dock, a voice calls:
"Jesus, are you to hell still *there?*
You want a drink or something?
God, it's the middle of the damned
*night,* I mean. Hey, do you *own*
this place? You can *have* it!
Jesus, what a weekend. . . . "

And from further up the headland,
off behind the unrestored museum:
"Phil-l-up! Come on! It's
*freezing!* We can't find the *car!*
What're you *doing?* come *on!*"

Well, I'm standing here,
where the dock said

"the hell with it,"
and I'm thinking.
Thinking. Whatever.
That Sherman didn't mean
what he said about Indians.
That Grant and Lee and
Meade and Sheridan
didn't stay to watch
the ghost-regiments
lay down their arms.
(But Longstreet did—the
tattered remains of Jackson's
1st Brigade marched past.
Never has a defeat in arms
been so tragic, won such
keen purity of pride. . . .

Poor Longstreet, who passed
up and down the flotsam shingle
on the beach alone, at Petoskey,
Michigan, and Harbor Springs,
south of Furnace Harbor,
watching the waves ride in,
curl, and suck away
On his northern, stone-wrung coast.
An American, a Michigan boy,
maybe he was Bruce Catton,
asked Longstreet, with tears
in his eyes, "Why, why, *why*
didn't you attack!" At
Cemetery Ridge. Longstreet
said "I did." And walked away.
North by west, toward
Furnace Harbor.

How our history weighs upon us,
includes us, like a drama
in which we are all the actors!
America is a catch in the throat

of all our lives. So young, for
so many tears. What history
do you see in the eyes
of a Dakota, boy or girl?
A Black, long freed from slavery?
Or the many generations
of the immigrants, alone?

*

And Roy, too, sailed
and sank, and rose
again . . . no, no he didn't.
Nor did he make it home,
nor were his wives waiting,
nor was he on real business,
nor did he paint an
archeological masterpiece
in Kindergarten Primitive.
Though become a poet of patterns,
obsessed with birdflight and
the dancing spots of the TV
(he scrambled his own satellite,
searching for the One, True Picture behind
the image), he remains father
only of his bell-rung desires.
*Exit* Roy, man of an hour.
Asleep tonight, belowdecks,
ironman curled tight in a
cot? No. Big man, broadly
fleshed, turned to in his berth,
guiltless in sleep, unforgiven,
a disappointed, weary
Jason, something heavy
in the heart. Dreaming?
Yes. Perhaps. Of the
Argonauts' wondrous
return home, to . . .
the fruits of sufficiency.
The laughter of women.

For everything turns, the buoy knows,
turns again, and always, again.
In that turning alone, we iron out
the ground of hope, keep love,
I think, thinking. And bay,
pineshadowed, limestone cliffs,
animal heard, in the bells
ringing, as the wind lifts . . .

*a pattern so intricate,*
*yet regular, yet incomplete,*
*no ear human or animal*
*may predict, or know, or escape*
*it, or count upon when*
*or whether the one dong*
*will echo the last one,*
*or the next, or the next,*
*or be the one, last one,*
*of all the first. . . .*

         Dong / dong   Dong   Dong / Dong
     Dong               Dong / dong

To mark the channel,
ride from Indian to ironmen
burial. And pray for nothing;
that will come. Will come.
To the rocking bell

       that rocks and cradles

       the hammering tongues

         of our passages.

## Poetry from Illinois